READY.SET. START!

Jonathan Bachew

Ready. Set. Start!

Copyright © 2018 by Jonathan Bachew

All rights reserved. No part of this publication may be reproduced, distributed, or transmitted in any form or by any means, including photocopying, recording, or any other electronic or mechanical methods, without the prior written permission of the publisher, except in the case of brief quotations embodied in critical reviews and certain other noncommercial uses permitted by copyright law. For permission requests, write to the publisher, at the address below.

Jonathan Bachew

Jonathanbachew@hotmail.com

Stockholm Sweden.

Ready. Set. Start!

WHAT YOU ARE ABOUT TO LEARN

When an Entrepreneur is succeeding in business, we usually see the tip of the iceberg. This tip of the iceberg is shiny, beautiful and attractive and many want to have it.

The success is evident to those around and can be seen with our eyes. This is great and serves as motivation and inspiration to others. The rest of the iceberg is submerged under the water and makes up a larger and more meaningful portion of the whole. I have written about the unseen parts of how to succeed. This is the mindset, the mentality, the motivations and the reasons behind Entrepreneurship.

When you learn the deeper meaning of what Entrepreneurship is about, the result is

Ready. Set. Start!

greater and longer lasting success. You will learn both the practical and theoretical things needed to be known when starting a business.

Ready. Set. Start!

DEDICATION

I dedicate this book to my wife Jhessicka Bachew. She is my number one supporter who has stuck by my side for 12 years. Through it all, she never wavered in her support and has always believed in my dreams. She is my inspiration, best friend and life partner. To my three children, I love you all very much.

To all my friends, supporters and family, thank you for the support over the years and for the encouragement.

To those who will read this book, I hope that your life will improve because of reading it.

Ready. Set. Start!

ABOUT THE AUTHOR

Jonathan Bachew, he has started small businesses over his lifetime and was very involved in nonprofit work. From a young age, he enjoyed the thrill of creating the 'lemon aid stand' and dreaming up business ideas. When Amazon.com was not as famous as it is today, he created a catalogue of items from their site, to be sold. It was a booklet filled with products, pictures, and descriptions. Most of who bought from it didn't have credit cards to buy from Amazon directly, so he was able to import and sell from the site. He was also a musical Entrepreneur, who wrote and produced music. He owned a studio and started a music school among other things. It took a lot of business and Entrepreneurial skills to keep that going and to help people in the process. Both he and his wife started a real estate company that they operated for some time. He has learned a lot about business and Entrepreneurship from hustling, sitting in the room with some major players, and learning from that experience.

They also started a non-profit organization that helps the community it is in, to improve the lives of the people living there. Entrepreneurship runs through his veins, and he loves the challenge of planning, mobilizing people and launching new things. His motivations were always to learn new things and help people improve their lives. His goal is to lead a movement of training, support and development for Entrepreneurs through books, online courses, seminars, conferences, and other educational resources.

Ready. Set. Start!

TABLE OF CONTENTS

WHAT YOU ARE ABOUT TO LEARN　　ii
DEDICATION　　iv
ABOUT THE AUTHOR　　v

SECTION 1: GETTING READY

CHAPTER 1: THE VALUE OF ENTREPRENEURSHIP　　1
CHAPTER 2: EMPLOYMENT　　8
CHAPTER 3: MOTIVATION AND MOTIVES　　22
CHAPTER 4: FREEDOM OF TIME　　31
CHAPTER 5: RETIREMENT　　40
CHAPTER 6: FINDING YOURSELF　　45
CHAPTER 7: THE THINGS WE LOVE　　55

SECTION 2: GETTING SET

CHAPTER 8: BUSINESS SCHOOL　　66
CHAPTER 9: THE DIFFERENT TYPES OF BUSINESSES　　73
CHAPTER 10: WHAT BUSINESS TO GET INTO　　82

Ready. Set. Start!

CHAPTER 11: MARKETS	88
CHAPTER 12: THE BUSINESS PLAN	97

SECTION 3: GETTING STARTED

CHAPTER 13: CONFIDENCE	114
CHAPTER 14: STEREOTYPES	126
CHAPTER 15: STARTING	133
CHAPTER 16: CONGRATULATIONS	142

SECTION 1

GETTING READY

CHAPTER 1

THE VALUE OF ENTREPRENEURSHIP

We need you! The world needs more Entrepreneurs. In my opinion, Entrepreneurship is the hero work because many people are helped and lifted through the contributions of Entrepreneurs.

National Economic Growth

The country that has many Entrepreneurs, usually see their economy positively affected as a result. By contrast, the countries that do not foster a healthy environment for Entrepreneurs to function in, usually suffer for it.

The countries that have high taxes and stifling regulations on small businesses are sending a message. The message is that they don't value and appreciate the contributions of Entrepreneurs.

The result is that more people are discouraged from starting a business. The high taxes and limitations placed by governments is a form of punishment.

They are punishing producers, dreamers, and major contributors. What governments are trying to accomplish by doing this is to create more dependency on their system. Their system is: go to school, become an employee for life, retire when old and then die.

This is their formula for life, and they will indirectly discourage anyone who has a different system. I believe that the governments that promote a healthy environment for Entrepreneurs within their countries benefit the most.

Small businesses and new businesses of all types bring fresh air and new vitality into an economy. Countries with more incentives, rewards, and lowering of crippling taxes on small businesses will benefit. It sends a message to the citizens that Entrepreneurship is valued, appreciated, rewarded and encouraged here.

Ready. Set. Start!

This will attract like-minded people, and the economic growth will be explosive. Entrepreneurship is an answer to poverty, rising crime and fewer jobs being available.

If you want to help people rise out of poverty and other socio-economic problems, educate them on Entrepreneurship. This book can be used to inspire and educate people on how to pull themselves out of unfavorable financial situations.

Every person you see struggling financially is not alone. If it is a husband, then there is a wife involved who is also struggling.

There may be children involved and elderly family members who are all in the financial difficulty. Helping one person out of their financial struggles usually means helping their entire families out of difficulties. Helping families means helping Communities too.

We can give someone a fish today and tomorrow they will be hungry again. We can teach someone to fish, and in time they may be able to find food every day. When we teach Entrepreneurship, we help empower people to pull themselves out of their financial situations. I hope to connect with like-minded people who desire to help people lift themselves out of the financial problems of high debt, running out of money before the month is finished and not having enough money to make ends meet. That is why I wrote this book and desire to write more in the future. I hope it gets into the hands of everyone who needs it.

Entrepreneurs are job creators. If you want more eggs, get a chicken. The chicken lays the eggs. If you want more jobs, encourage Entrepreneurship. Entrepreneurs create the jobs. Many of the people who have been given a job and a chance to work are employed or active because of Entrepreneurs.

The Entire economy functions on having jobs created and jobs available. The best Entrepreneurs create jobs for others. Entrepreneurship is, therefore, a noble and essential service to the Economy.

Jobs are important

The world needs millions of Jobs. The economy needs many people who can go to work so our society can function. We need nurses, doctors, carpenters, managers, construction workers, shop workers, healthcare professionals, designers, writers, factory workers, transportation workers, and salespeople. We need many various types of jobs in the economy.

Entrepreneurship is not about attacking the concept of 'having a job.' The opposite is true. Entrepreneurship is about valuing the creation of jobs. Entrepreneurs create the jobs that help families put food on their table and help people make a living. Think of the millions of people worldwide who can provide for their families because of their job. Think of how many job opportunities you can create someday. How many people can find employment and contribute meaningfully to society because of your business? Think of the value that the job holds to an employee.

Many people in the future are depending on you to create jobs. Their future employment, meaningful contributions to society and avenues to express themselves is dependent on your actions today.

We hear of companies closing resulting in many people losing their jobs, negatively affecting families, personal dreams and hopes. Entrepreneurs have a great responsibility in creating job stability and confidence in the economy. We cannot depend on governments to create stable economies, we need more empowered Entrepreneurs.

We need more jobs in society, but jobs alone should not be the whole financial plan. A job should be a financial foundation until a person can graduate into the world of Entrepreneurship. People must decide if they want to be an Entrepreneur, work in a job or do some of both. Nothing is wrong with either of the two. Just be true to yourself and to your personal passions and interests. If a job excites you and gives you a sense of purpose, then be true to yourself. If the thought of business ownership excites you and gives you purpose, then be true to yourself. We must all be true to ourselves and to what inspires us.

Some people may not be excited about Entrepreneurship because they do not understand the benefits of it. I will say that the worlds of Employment and Entrepreneurship are different and provide different levels of freedom. I will describe the advantages and disadvantages of having a job throughout the book. Jobs are an important foundational part of our economy. Most entrepreneurs started

Ready. Set. Start!

off working at a job before becoming an Entrepreneur.

In our society, we need both. Sam Walton was one of the Best Entrepreneurs. He created the Business system called Walmart. Walmart currently employs 2.1 million people. Think of the many families financially affected.

In the United States alone, the company employs 1.4 million people. This is an astounding 1% of the U.S.'s 140 million working population. I can only imagine the total amount of people who were employed throughout its lifetime. That's the power of one Entrepreneur! One Entrepreneur has the potential to positively affect the lives of more people than we could imagine.

Every size and type of business has the potential to create various jobs. Entrepreneurs are opportunity creators, dream creators and make contributions that improve the standard of living to millions.

CHAPTER 2

EMPLOYMENT

Let's talk about employment

Employment is when a person is paid for the use of their time, energies, labor and skill. They trade their skills, intelligence or labor for a salary and they work for an employer who hires them. Employment can be fulfilling and meaningful to some.

Most people have been taught and trained to have a job. The school system is not designed to create entrepreneurs, it is designed to create employees. Every person has a set of needs and bills that must be met each month, so it's essential to have enough cash flow each month to support your lifestyle. The

Ready. Set. Start!

Educational system teaches people that the way to have money is to work at a job.

For those desiring the leave the world of employment and enter the world of self-employment, you need to think about financially supporting your lifestyle. If your lifestyle cannot be supported by a new start-up business, then I recommend keeping your job a bit longer. Being an Entrepreneur is not about being foolish. Do not leave your job and be put out on the streets because you can't pay your house mortgage etc.

If you are serious about being an Entrepreneur, then you must create a bridge from the world of Employment to the world of Self-employment. While one foot is in the world of employment, diligently and deliberately build your business on the side. When your new business has gained momentum and is generating a healthy cash flow, then you may leave the world of employment.

Ready. Set. Start!

Employability

Employability is what most people spend their life gaining. They go to school from an early age, complete high school and then some move on to college. All of this is preparation for becoming employed. Being employable is not the same as being employed. Some Entrepreneurs are not employed, but they are employable. Employability means that you can be employed if so desired. For most people, studying and preparing for a job is the only financial path they understand. I think this is a good start, but not the whole picture. I see employability as a foundation and not the whole house. Being an Entrepreneur does not mean being anti-jobs.

It is a very common thing to see some Entrepreneurs being completely Anti-Job. A job can be useful for transitioning and learning. My advice – Be a brilliant Entrepreneur and be employable. That way you are ready for any possible outcome. I remember having a discussion with my Dad years ago. We were discussing a certain subject, and I remember saying to him a few times, "I'll be ready for any possible outcome." Hearing myself say that, has stuck in my mind for some reason.

In writing this chapter, I hear the words "be ready for any possible outcome." The reasoning behind being ready for anything stems from the thought: "I don't want to be a slave to anything." If a career path is no longer what I need to do at that season in life, I want the freedom to leave. If I know that I'm supposed to be doing something, I want the freedom to go do it. I want the Freedom to choose what I do. Not having options is a real problem that people face. People who do not have options are stuck, and that's one of the worst feelings. They are at a job, not because of choice, but out of need. The goal is to get to a place, where, whatever you do is not because of need, but because of choice. It's a lifelong process that must be a deliberately set goal.

The lifelong goal should be to create many options, so you can flourish anywhere. If a person must work at a job, they should flourish there. If a person starts a business, they should flourish there. I want to develop my knowledge and experience to such a depth, that whatever I touch turns to Gold. No matter what I decide to use my hands to do.

Ready. Set. Start!

Your Job

If you are currently employed, I believe that you must give your job the fair amount of attention, it deserves. Do not neglect your job responsibilities and become distracted. Put in the fair number of hours and diligence that you are being paid for. Getting ready to start a business is not an excuse to become lazy at the job.

To be an Entrepreneur you must have an amazing work ethic, and if you slack off, at the job, you destroy your own character. That lack of character becomes part of the foundation of your new business and may be negatively affected by that choice. One day you will have employees working for you, and you want to show them, by example, that having a good attitude and work ethic is important.

Your business startup

Do not neglect your business because of the job. Give each it's fair and deserving time and attention. The Business represents your future, and you want to build it well. There must be a healthy balance between job and business, before the transition.

Remember that the job is someone else's business and your business is your business. When you have started your business, and it begins to generate enough cash flow, to support your lifestyle, then you have the option to leave the job or to continue the two. If leaving the job is the best choice for the health and growth of your business, Go full time into your business.

The main point is to have options. It comes down to your core values and who you are on the inside. The ideal reason for having a job should be to learn. It is wise to have certain jobs at times- for learning. You can learn how the system works and what works within an industry. The gained experience is what you are after.

You can learn from great Entrepreneurial mentors at work that can add value to your life. Working with an entrepreneur in building his/her business is an excellent training. You can get a front row seat to how a great Entrepreneur is building the business and learn from that mentorship.

The important thing is that you are learning deliberately. But, why are you learning? To what Ultimate goal? All your life's learning should eventually culminate into a specific use. You must find out what that is. I have worked in jobs just for learning specific things from that job, for the ultimate goal of learning how to be a better Entrepreneur.

The Two-sided Coin

A job is a two-sided Coin. There is a good side to a job. That is the side where a person can earn for their family, pay their bills and make ends meet. There is another face of the coin. This is the side of a job that many teachers of Entrepreneurship focus on. There is a dark side to employment.

A job has its limitations

Most people cannot become rich from a job because it is not designed for that purpose. It is designed for basic survival and not for abundance.

Ready. Set. Start!

Time

A job is not designed to give you freedom of time. A job is designed to use as much of your time as possible.

Distraction

If you have a business startup that is taking off and doing well, it will demand more time and attention. The job may become a distraction from your promising business. There will come a crossroad where you must take the leap of faith and leave the job.

Illusion of security

A job creates a beautiful illusion. An illusion means that something is not being entirely truthful. In most places in the world, having a job is risky. Every day we hear of companies closing, thousands of workers losing their jobs and being left unemployed. Job security is becoming a thing of the past. Long ago people felt confident in knowing that

Ready. Set. Start!

the company they worked for will employ them for life. You already know that's not the case anymore.

In today's world, things are changing much too quickly. Humanity is also in a silent competition with the thing they love, Technology. Millions of jobs have been replaced by technology already, and millions are expected to be replaced by automation soon. Not long ago in schools, there was a class for learning to type. Many schools had a room full of typewriters. Students in that class were preparing for a job as a typist, and there were millions around the world preparing for this job.

The only way, back then, to have a document typed was with a typewriter. There was a huge demand for people with this skill. People seeing this demand got excited and headed for job security. When the computer advanced in technology, everyone was able to type their own documents at home and print it. This one development completely eradicated the demand for this job (working with a typewriter). This is one small example of a much larger reality, happening every day.

Ready. Set. Start!

Many people are studying and preparing themselves for 6 years or more for a job that will no longer exist. They will have a certificate, a degree and a lot of knowledge about something that is no longer needed. Eric Hoffer said, "In times of change, learners inherit the earth, while the learned find themselves beautifully equipped to deal with a world that no longer exists." Many people today belong to jobs that will be erased entirely from the market. Their heads are in the sand, and they don't want to see the reality. They hope it will all go away. Placing their head in the sand won't affect the tidal wave approaching.

Unfortunately, In the march of progress, many will be trampled. Job security is a term that must be used carefully because many people do not have it.

Real Job security

There are a few people who have real job security. They can be rest assured that their job is safe and secure. I saw a movie of an airplane carrying prisoners. The airplane was a flying prison, and there were men in chains, being

Ready. Set. Start!

transported from one prison facility to another. One man, in particular, was heavily guarded. He had extra security guards, with larger guns assigned to him. He was chained with larger chains and had a muzzle and a face mask. He seemed to have more security than a leader of a country.

The more security given to him the more of a prisoner he was. That's the reality of security. The more a person has security, the more of a prisoner they become. Those with Job security are usually chained to that job. These people feel like slaves in their offices and titles. They must work and cling to that security for their dear life, even if they dislike their job, they must stay there to feel safe. People who are climbing the corporate ladder are trying to go higher up for the perceived security. They think that the higher they climb and the bigger the title or position, the safer they will be. Even if it means trampling others on the way up, or having their values twisted, they do it for the security.

I remember watching the cartoon Aladdin. The Genie was describing his situation to Aladdin. He said of himself "Phenomenal power….. itsy bitsy living space." The genie was huge and magnificent and had so much power, yet he had to go back into his little lamp. Some of these secure people have big titles, lots of power and influence.

They may be famous or have a lot of things. However, their world is tiny. It comes down to what motivates a person. When people are motivated by the fear of losing their job, they choose Security. They will have to pay a high price for that security because they never try anything else.

Entrepreneurs are motivated by freedom. The fewer security guards, chains, fences, guard dogs, burglar proofing and security cameras, the more freedom they feel. They may not be as big and flashy as someone with a big job title, but their world is a lot bigger.

My advice is to use employment as a temporary step and make becoming an Entrepreneur the long-term goal. I want everyone to learn about the value of Entrepreneurship so that they can be all that they were made to be. The possibilities of financial freedom, freedom of time, financial independence and the satisfaction that comes with it, is worth it. I believe that anyone can become an Entrepreneur and be financially free with the right attitude, determination, and know-how, it is possible. The ultimate vision is to one day become a fulltime, all in, business owner.

Discovering Entrepreneurship

Starting a Business is like building a house. If someone has a desire to build a house, he must understand that it will be a process. A process means that things must be done in an orderly fashion and in the correct order. First things first, second things second, etc. Imagine that there are 20 things to be done in building a house. It cannot be done randomly but must be done in chronological order.

Let's think of the alphabet for example. No one sings B, G, D, Y, W, X, G, H. Yes, these are indeed letters of the alphabet, but the alphabet also has an alphabetical order. This means that there is a first letter, the last letter, and letters in between, placed in a specific order. A is first, B is second, C is third, D is fourth, etc.

Having ideas about what is needed to start your business is not enough. These ideas must

Ready. Set. Start!

be organized into a step by step process. This book has been designed to lay out the needed steps in an order. I hope that you follow the steps from the first chapter to the last chapter and walk through the process of starting a business.

CHAPTER 3

MOTIVATION AND MOTIVES

Motivation

Entrepreneurs must be motivated.

They must have enough motivation for themselves.

They must have motivation to share with those who work with them.

They must have motivation to share with their customers.

The Entrepreneur needs a constant supply of motivation.

What is Motivation?

Having desire and stimulation to maintain interest in accomplishing a goal. It's having 'steam in the engine.' There are different levels of intensity of motivation.

When there is a task at hand, some are not motivated for the task, some may be barely motivated for a task and others may be highly motivated for a task.

To start and run a business an Entrepreneur will need a lot of motivation because there will be a lot of challenges to face and many problems to be solved. There will be up and down moments, and there will be things that will want to stand in the way of success. Therefore, an Entrepreneur must understand the science of motivation.

Drive

When something is driven, it is moved or influenced by energy pushing against it. Movement is only created by energy pushing against something. You need to be internally driven, pushed and full of energy.

Ready. Set. Start!

Locomotive

A locomotive is an engine powered railway vehicle used for pulling trains. The word originates from the two Latin words

1. Loco – "From a place."
2. Motivus – "Causing motion."

The resulting word is Locomotive which means- Creating motion to go from one place to another place. The way names contain a description of the nature of a thing is incredible

Automotive

This is a vehicle propelled by a self-contained motor, engine, or the like. It is originated from two words.

1. Auto - means 'self'
2. Motive - creating motion

We can see from the examples that the word 'Motive' means A driving force that causes something to move. The original word for 'Motive' is the same word that makes the word for 'Motivation.'

Ready. Set. Start!

In today's world, we use the word 'motivation' to describe drive, energy or passion and we use the word 'motive' to describe reason or purpose. Both words had the same meaning originally and were inseparable.

The way to be Motivated is to have healthy Motives because motives create motivation. Motives are the reasons for doing something and motivation is the power to do it. Have control over your motives, and you have control over your motivation. Many people rely on receiving a daily handout of motivation from others. It is good to receive motivation from others, but this should be a secondary source. It is better to learn how to create it than to receive it.

The primary source of motivation must come from within yourself. True entrepreneurs are self-motivated people. It is not realistic or healthy to expect people to show up with a handout of motivation every time we feel de-motivated.

When we need motivation, we should be able to muster it from the inside. It's like making a cake every day. Instead of asking the neighbors for flour, butter, and sugar every day, it's wiser to have a full cupboard of the ingredients in your house. That way you can just reach over get the ingredients from your own supply and bake yourself a cake. What if someday the neighbor doesn't have salt or sugar?

Then you would have to go without valuable ingredients, and that's not an option. Entrepreneurship is built on a desire to not have an unhealthy and unrealistic dependence on others. Depending on others to stay motivated is for followers, not leaders.

Motives

Motives are the reasons behind action. Why are you doing something? You must carefully search yourself and list your motives.

Why are you in business?

What do you hope to achieve?

What is most important to you in life?

Why do you need money?

Why not just be an employee?

Why be an entrepreneur?

Why is it important to succeed?

Ready. Set. Start!

What does success mean to you?

Why should you create value for customers?

Why do you exist?

Why are you alive?

Before you go any further, pause and write down all your motives and reasons for everything. Your reason for living, your reason for wanting to be in business and your reason for being goal oriented, etc.

Motives can be difficult to locate. For some reason, motives reside in a place within us that is vague and cloudy. It's not easy to identify the Big why's, but the good news is that it is possible to find them. Search long and hard, and you can receive more information on this in the chapter called Finding yourself.

Great Entrepreneurs have motives such as

To add value to others

To provide for their family and loved ones

To make a difference

To do what they love

To utilize all their potential in life

To be true to themselves

To overcome fear and limitations

Ready. Set. Start!

To find a better way to live

To solve problems

To not have to work for money their whole lives

To retire young

To have enough money to do the things they love to do

To not be a slave to anything

To not be a slave to anyone

To be Free

To have freedom

To be independent

To not have to depend on others to determine their quality of life.

People can perform the very same act. For example, two people may start a business. The starting of a business is the same activity that both people perform. These two people may have different motives. One person wants a business to make fast money and get rich quick. The other person may have the motive of adding value to others over a period of time.

Two different motives, the same act. The act is not as important as the motive. People think that if they do the same things the rich do, they will become rich as well. They think if they start a business, that act is enough to make them succeed. The act of starting a business is not what causes success. The quality of the motives is what determines success.

Fuel

There are different qualities of fuel. Some fuel is made of poor quality and will only drive a vehicle for a certain distance. Some fuels are of average quality and will drive a vehicle for a little more distance, while some fuels are of high quality and can drive a vehicle for long distances.

Motives are fuels

Each motive is a different quality of fuel. Some motives have the power to take you only so far in your journey. Other motives have the power to take you on a very far journey. Motives Create Motivation so, therefore, your 'why' creates your ability to last.

Here are some poor-quality fuels (motives)

Ready. Set. Start!

I need everyone to like me

I don't want to embarrass myself.

It's the trendy thing to do

Everybody is doing it

I have no other choice

It sounds like a good idea

I must never fail

Making mistakes is bad

People may think badly of me

I just need the money

What if people stop liking me?

What would others think?

One of the main reasons for failure is caring too much about what people think. The good news is that we can customize and remake the reasons why we do things. We can replace a faulty motive with a better one.

Find all your faulty motives and replace them with better ones. Attempting to be free is more important than worrying about what others may think. For those who have lost their motivation, they may have just lost their "Why." Go get it back!

CHAPTER 4

FREEDOM OF TIME

There was a rich man who had 50 billion dollars in the bank. He was very old and on his death bed. Just before his last breath an angel appeared and said, "I will give you 50 more years of life if you pay me 50 billion dollars".

What do you think the dying man's response was?

"Of course,"!!The rich man knows that he can always regain that money over time and besides, what good is money if you have no time? Money is replaceable, but time isn't.

Time is the most valuable thing. The richest man on earth cannot buy a single minute more of life in his last moments. The richest men in the history of the world are gone

Ready. Set. Start!

and mostly forgotten. What good was all that money? Their time ran out. Time says, "Game start," and same Time says, "Game over." Time is the thing of real value.

Entrepreneurs have strong values. They want more time to spend doing what is important to them, without being told otherwise. They want more time to do the things they love to do. They want the free time to travel the world. They want to be free to enjoy hobbies like art, painting, photography, visiting museums all over the world, etc.

Most of these desires remain only dreams that never becomes a reality for many people. Many people start businesses with the hope of freedom. Freedom to control what they do with their time. Freedom to not have to work in a job for the rest of their lives.

They believe that all the years they used working in a job, that they don't enjoy, is the time they could have been used on something else.

There are some who love to volunteer in a non-profit, or in a religious organization. They may have dreams of spending much more time in their house of worship, serving people and the cause. They dream of having enough money to donate to their church or favorite charity, but they are very busy at their job and wish they had more time to give towards volunteering, etc.

This creates an inner tension of not being able to do more with their limited time. The best Entrepreneurs don't start businesses just for the money.

Paper Money

When I was a child, I remember going to a summer camp where campers would receive little paper tickets that had a value of one. One of what currency? You may ask, was it one dollar? One Yuan? One Sterling pound? One cryptocurrency. One of what? None of the above, just one paper ticket. Campers would receive those paper tickets for good behavior, doing chores, winning in sports activities, etc.

I remember kids not doing their chores, and when they were threatened with not getting tickets, they turned into the best workers. They magically turned into little angels for that paper. When the camp was

Ready. Set. Start!

almost over, all the kids could go buy from a wide variety of toys and gadgets, and it was a frenzy.

The tickets weren't even money, just paper, yet we could have bought so many things that had some perceived value. That's what money is. It is nothing on its own, it's just a representation of something else.

Did you catch that?

It represents - something else.

What is your 'something else'?

It's not about money, it's really about something else.

Do you know what that 'something else' is?

The same 1-dollar bill, if thrown in a fire, will turn to the same ashes as a 100-dollar bill. I don't know what costs more to make, a 100 dollar note or toilet paper. What I do know is that they are both paper. Today money isn't even paper, it is just an idea. It represents what we shake hands on. Money is just some numbers that exist in a digital banking system. It is electrical signals flying around inside a computer, creating an image on a screen. It's not even a physical thing anymore, its digital.

Ready. Set. Start!

A Dictator

A dictator is a political leader who possesses absolute power. The tyrant places many limitations and restrictions to those under his rule. Dictators have a reputation for taking away liberties and freedoms. They thrive on manipulating and controlling the minds of people. The people live in a controlled and prison-like system where they have lesser freedoms and rights.

The main characteristic of a dictatorship is the lack of Freedom. People live in constant fear and in an unhealthy dependency on the Dictator. Their lives are built around not losing favor with the Dictator.

To most people in the world, the lack of money is a dictator. The lack of money dictates their every move and their every choice. They cannot do anything without first consulting the dictator. If they desire something, they must see if they can afford it. 'I cannot afford it' is the sentence used by someone who lives under the dictatorship.

Money wants to dictate, what a person's limits are in every aspect of their lives. It dictates the limits of how much food can be bought at the grocery store. Instead of buying a $1000 sofa it dictates that they can only buy the $500 sofa. Instead of buying the pack of 100 diapers, it dictates that they can only afford to buy the 20 pack.

It dictates the limit of what car they drive.

It dictates what they do with their time.

It dictates when and what they do for satisfaction.

It dictates whether some people get married or not.

It dictates the quality of education some can receive.

It dictates when a person can travel.

It dictates if they can travel.

It dictates where they can travel to.

It dictates what type of house someone can buy.

It dictates whether someone can even have their own house or not. It dictates how many hours a person must spend at work. It dictates what someone can afford and what they cannot afford. It dictates if you can pursue a dream or not.

Ready. Set. Start!

Those with a lack of money feel confined, limited, restricted and a lack of freedom. The lack of money is a dictator. It's about time to have time!

The best Entrepreneurs start businesses, to make money, to buy time. To buy the ability to decide what time in the morning they can awake. To decide for themselves when they can go travel to another part of the world or visit that dream destination. Slavery is about not having freedom. Freedom and slavery are exact opposite concepts. When someone does not have the freedom to do the things they truly enjoy, they will sense this within themselves.

The struggle to be free

When someone tries to break free, there will be an initial struggle, but the dictator will suppress the uprising and rebellion. Some continue in the struggle to be free and never give up. They only stop the fight when they have achieved freedom. Some others give up on the struggle for freedom. They have tried to be free, but the fight is fierce and long, and after some time, they choose to settle. They

Ready. Set. Start!

think that they are at peace because they are no longer in a struggle, but they have given up. Most people can only go on vacations at certain times of the year because they must work.

Entrepreneurs dream of having the freedom to do whatever they want, whenever they want to. That's what people are hoping to buy with the money they get. It's not really about the money. The money is the middle man and if it were possible to remove the middleman, many would, but the middleman is always there. It's about the ability to buy the control of your time.

Now some people may absolutely love their job. It's their dream and the perfect use of their time. That's great. Some people love their job schedule and think that nothing else really matters. If that suits them, wonderful.

There are people however that do not enjoy the conventional concept of a job. Eighty-five percent of workers worldwide admit to disliking their jobs when surveyed anonymously, according to a recent poll.

For many, a large portion of their days is spent at work; in fact, the average person will spend 90,000 hours at work over a lifetime. That is one-third of their life being spent on a job. A job is not designed to give a person freedom of time. I believe that becoming an entrepreneur, starting your own business and investing in income-producing assets, is the way to financial freedom and the freedom to control your time.

Ready. Set. Start!

CHAPTER 5

RETIREMENT

Retirement is a complex topic. You can hire an advisor whose job is solely educating about retirement. Some countries see retirement as a right, and others don't. Each country has their own retirement age. For example, the retirement age in France and the USA is 62-67, In Peru it's 60. This is in 2018.

The ideological and political battles are fierce on the topic.

The Young

Some young people think that they don't have to worry about retirement. They think they have enough time to think about it later.

The Middle-Aged

Ready. Set. Start!

Many people in their midlife, start to think more seriously about retirement.

The Older years

Many people in their older years are forced to live with the reality of retirement. There are those whose retirement plan is to retire when they are old. Many people on retirement, must lower their standard of living, considerably. They may sell their home and buy a smaller place to live and cut down on what they spend money on. Their budget must be remade to fit their new limited income. Their health and physical bodies are no longer the same as when they were younger. After they have worked their entire lives and gotten a lot older, they are now ready to start enjoying life. Retirement is one of the most frightening things to a lot of people.

Here are some things people are afraid of

-Running out of money during retirement years.

-The ups and downs of the economy.

-Having regrets about financial decisions made earlier in life.

-Sudden and unplanned expenses.

-Medical bills.

Ready. Set. Start!

-Being trapped and immobilized by a small income.

-Having no more time to make meaningful financial changes.

My advice to younger people is to try all you possibly can to retire as early as possible. Make it a life struggle. There is always something on the inside of an Entrepreneur that is fighting to be free from the need to retire at an old age. Retirement, for me, means having enough money to pay for your lifestyle, without having to work. Some people can retire young. Those who retire young have, potentially, many years ahead to enjoy their life and see the world.

I have always wondered, what if someone has worked hard their entire lives, used all their precious hours in a job, and just when they are about to begin enjoying their life, at retirement, they die. It's sad but happens.

I know that many must work hard their whole lives and retire when they are older because it's just a reality of the current system, but what if someone can retire young. What if someone can have reasonable youth left in them to run, play and visit those wonderful

Ready. Set. Start!

destinations with their loved ones. This is a dream for many. I believe that Entrepreneurship is the path to the dream of retiring young. It's a form of rebellion against the common rules.

The rules say —You must work your entire life and retire when you are possibly in the last years of your life. You must use all your valuable, young and middle age years, at a job. This is quite unsettling to some. I believe that a person must at least try. At least while you are still young and physically can still try. A person can hustle and try their very best to break that rule.

There are people in our world who are retiring young and don't have to wait till they are old. They have invested in a business or real estate, and those assets will support them.

Entrepreneurship is the way to retire young. Starting a business that can grow over time and creating enough cash flow, is the goal. I know there will come a time when we are old and cannot work anymore due to age, but while there is still some youth in you, get out there and try to make the dream of early retirement a reality.

Ready. Set. Start!

While you are attempting this dream, be sure to create a safety net for retirement in your old age.

Don't give up the fight.

CHAPTER 6

FINDING YOURSELF

Imagine there is a bar of gold that is very valuable. It is placed on the floor and glistens in the sunlight because it is pure, clean and full of worth. Along comes a truck and empties its tray, filled with sand, on top of it. The golden bar is still there, it is just covered by the mountain of sand.

To find the gold we need to dig deep and search for it. A person is valuable and is represented by the golden bar. In life, things get dumped onto us that can cover up the actual person that we are on the inside. We all have things about us that are special, unique and truly who we are but over the years of life, we can be covered by some things.

Ready. Set. Start!

Depressing situations

Some people go through many unfortunate things. Their life has been a story of tragedy, loss and other issues and these things may cover a person in depression. Some may have come from depressing family situations, neighborhoods, and countries where there are high levels of crime and poverty. A person will have to fight to rise out of it. There are many other instances of feeling buried in tough life situations. The fight may have been an internal one, dealing with emotional turmoil and anxieties.

People's expectations of us

There are people in our lives who are very influential in shaping our view of ourselves. When we try to please them, sometimes it comes at a price of no longer being true to ourselves. They can be friends, family members, teachers or people we respect. Sometimes the expectations placed on us causes us to warp and bend out of our true shape.

Ready. Set. Start!

Feelings of fear and insecurities

Deep down we are all brave, amazing and confident people. As we go through life, we will face hardships and difficulties. These tough times can cause us to retreat into a shell of fear and a cave of insecurity. We may begin to doubt ourselves and forget who we truly are.

The temporary failures and defeats are sometimes turned in to lifelong definitions of who we are. This is an example of a golden bar, being buried by sand. Some take what was meant to be a stepping stone and turn it into a tombstone. Failure is not meant to be final, get up and try again and again. Each attempt more intelligently than the last.

Wanting to fit into society

Society is like a huge Molding machine. A mold is a device that presses and forms a material into a desired shape. There are many powerful systems in our world that are designed to create copies and prints of people. Many people are born into these powerful systems that press people into thinking, behaving and living a certain way.

We must identify the molding machines that are at work, trying to make everyone think and act the same way. This is important because we are all unique and different and should be able to have that freedom to express our individuality. One small example of this is the mold of having everyone believe that they must, go to school, get a job, pay bills, retire when old then die. Many people will change their identity and their true selves to fit into that mold. They don't want to stand out as being strange, weird or an outcast.

The desire for social acceptance and to be welcomed into certain circles of people, can cause some people to pretend to be something they are not. Over many years of acting and playing the role, a person can get lost in the role. They may forget who they truly are on the inside because they have pretended for so long. I saw a video of a pet parrot who grew up with dogs from his birth. The parrot barks like a dog and has imitated the dogs his whole life. He doesn't even know he is a parrot, he just repeats what he has seen and learned. Some people only do things because it is what they have seen and heard for a long time. They do not think for themselves and do not stand up for what they believe on the inside. They can be so much more, but are buried by everyone else's thoughts, and have forgotten their own thoughts.

Struggling for survival

Many people are brilliant, driven, intelligent and have desires to succeed in accomplishing great things. However, they are stuck in a cycle of Survival. Their need for the basics in life keeps them running around in circles. Some people feel a deep sense of desperation and find themselves acting and living in Survival mode. If the financial desperation and survival mode is removed, it will amaze everyone to see how much incredible things they can accomplish.

Survival and desperation can twist and change a person. In this category are some people who work in certain careers not because they love it but to survive. They must pay the bills, pay their debts, have a roof over their heads and have food to eat. This can keep people in a rat race, and they can lose their most real self. Many people are in a certain type of career or business for reasons other than it being what they love. They may have inherited a longstanding family tradition or got into a career because it was the only available option at the time of choosing. These are poor reasons for being involved in something for the long term.

Take time off

In some circles, people take time off to fast or abstain from certain things to increase their focus. Other people choose to meditate and examine their inner thoughts, and some go off on a journey of self-discovery. Others may use various methods, but the objective is to get away from distractions and do a deep soul searching. I want you to take time off to find yourself. This means getting alone, finding a quiet space and asking yourself hard questions as to why you do the things you do.

The goal is to remove the sand that has been dumped on you and find the golden bar of the true you. Think deeply about your life, past experiences, and your future.

See which mode you are on. Survival mode, thriving mode, fear mode, reacting mode. Search your deepest desires such as

What matters most to you?

Why are you involved in certain fields of employment and study?

Are you under any pressure from friends, family or society to be something?

Are you truly happy?

Are you completely free to be yourself?

If you could choose any career path or business venture, without the need for money, approval or acceptance what would it be? If you had the perfect courage and was free from all fear, what would you do? If you had 1 billion dollars and didn't need money, what would you do with your time?

What makes you come alive?

What makes your soul awakened and satisfied?

Why does your life schedule look the way it does?

Ready. Set. Start!

Why are you busy with those things right now?

Who are the most influential people in your life?

Are they influential by your choice or did you not have a choice in the matter? Is there someone whose approval you desire? Do you find yourself in certain systems of behavior and thinking that limit your growth? Are you free to question things? Are you punished for questioning things? Are people being set free to be themselves without the fear of judgment, within that system?

Are you a free person?

Are you a happy person?

Are you free to chase your deepest dreams without being ridiculed, judged, discouraged or abandoned? Do these things cause you to retreat from attempting your dreams?

Who are you really?

Who does everyone think you are? Why?

What is the public image you have created? Is that who you are when you are alone? If you realize that you need to make a major life change, what is stopping you from doing it?

Ready. Set. Start!

I believe that the people who succeed in business are those who are doing what they love. Doing what you love will give you the extra motivation you need. When you do what you love, it's no longer "work." You are being paid for something that you are passionate about.

One major reason for finding yourself is so that you can understand what makes you come alive. Choose a business path that is in line what who you truly are on the inside. If you love traveling the world, you may want to consider a business in that. If you believe deeply in certain products that have helped you personally, then that would be a good fit.

I love to teach and help people rise to higher levels. I also love the subject of business and Entrepreneurship and so it's a very natural and fulfilling thing for me to be involved in this field. What do you passionately and naturally share with people? Maybe create a business in line with that passion.

The ultimate goal is being free to be yourself, and this applies to everything in your life. In a smaller way, it applies to making life career choices. When choosing a life in business, choose something that is an accurate

Ready. Set. Start!

reflection of you, your desires and your dreams. Choose a business path in something that you love and have a natural passion for.

CHAPTER 7

THE THINGS WE LOVE

I always emphasize the importance of having a business in something you love. I have so far addressed the things you love as it relates to business, but business isn't everything and work isn't everything.

The meaning for life is not business and work. Meaning in life is giving attention and time to everything that you love.

Balance.

Our business is only one thing that we love. Business and working hard is a way to take care of all the things that are important us. In business, we take excellent care of our customers who we value and cherish. Other people in our lives are not customers that we take care of, and who are not related to the business. We all dream of doing more with the ones we love.

Your family

Work should be a part of our lives and not our whole life. We don't want to give everything we have to work alone, we must have something to give to our families.

Your family is more important than your work. The value and importance of your family is greater.

It's about priorities.

Many things in life are important, however, everything is not equally important. There is a hierarchy of importance. Business and work are important, but not more important than family. Even though we know that family is important, the reality for many is that it takes a lot of work to care for a family. It costs a lot of money to have a family and so, we must work hard.

Many people are working hard, in a job they dislike, to be able to provide for their family. The system of work and employment is designed to utilize the most valuable and

Ready. Set. Start!

productive times of our days. Most people will work Monday to Friday and even weekends using the best hours of the day and the best days of the week in their job. They get paid a salary in return, and with what energy is left, they are sent home with that. This is how our world is designed, and the masses, the billions of people on our planet has grown to accept it. It is a very noble, loving and responsible thing to be able to provide for your family. It should be the goal of every responsible person. Most people are taught that the only way they can nobly provide for their family, is to go to work.

Family members are very understanding of the realities of life.

Everyone knows that there are bills to be paid.

Mortgage payments to be made

Credit card debts to pay

Clothes to buy

Food to buy

Activities to pay for

A gym subscription to keep alive

A car loan payment to maintain

A savings for that annual vacation

Ready. Set. Start!

Medical bills

And the list goes on

Children are not usually disappointed that they cannot be with mommy or daddy as often as they like. They have all grown to accept this reality. Mommy and daddy are not as concerned about the amount of time and attention they can give their kids. They have been trained and taught by society to accept this as the norm.

We just bury it and move on.

It's just life

We accept it because we are taught that:

Everyone must pay this price.

Everyone has to sacrifice.

Everyone must work.

Everyone must use their best hours of the day at a job.

We have gotten used to the thought that working is just a normal part of life and it's just the way it is.

Entrepreneurs are different.

Entrepreneurs are not satisfied with this.

Entrepreneurs do not want this to be their life story.

Ready. Set. Start!

Entrepreneurs want an escape out of the rat race.

Entrepreneurs want to find a way out of this broad road filled with billions of marching people. The masses are noble, good, hardworking people and they sacrificially walk down this road, but the entrepreneur wants to find another way. Entrepreneurs want to be able to have the freedom to give more time and attention to their families.

Entrepreneurs seek freedom. Business is also hard work. Business also has demands on your time and attention but what makes a business different from a job, is that the demands don't have to last forever. A business has the potential to grow and create passive income.

The business can mature giving the entrepreneur increased freedom to be with the ones he loves. If you desire to have more time in the future for your family

Then become an Entrepreneur because Entrepreneurs value the dream of Freedom. Everything said about family can be said about friends. In my list of priorities, my friendships are just below my family. I value my friends, and true friends are hard to find. Sometimes, people want what you have or want to get a position or title.

The true friends are those who care about you and not just the things you have etc. Most people value their friendships and want more time to invest in their social network. Entrepreneurs seek the freedom to spend time with their friends.

I spoke about doing what you love as it relates to your business, your customers, your family, and friends, but there are other things that a person love. Something else that people love is the desire within themselves. You can call it hobbies, interests, desires, fascinations.

Basically, things you like.

Most people sacrifice the things that make them happy because they just don't have the time, energy and attention to give to it. It's just not possible with their current schedule.

One sad reality is that people go through painful and mournful burial ceremonies on the inside. They had a lifelong passion but must now grow up and put an end to it. They have no choice but to put the things they love, to rest. They lay at night and sob as they make

Ready. Set. Start!

that decision to no longer feel love for an interest. Something that meant a lot to them must be let go of. They had a lifelong dream or desire, and they are now faced with the truth that they may never be able to have it. People have grown up to the realities of the adult world and have learned to accept it. They believe that dreams are for kids and real adults cannot have dreams, yet we all have dreams, desires, and interests within ourselves

Here are a few

Blogging, Horse riding, Bungee jumping, Fishing, Visiting family and friends in another country, Acting, Hunting ,Archery, Calligraphy ,Photography, Travelling, Writing a book, Reading books, Baking, Scrap booking, Flower arranging, Gardening, Farming, Taking care of animals, Visiting exotic islands, Meeting new people, Learning a foreign language, Water sports ,Winter sports, Cross country biking, Cross country trekking, Migrating to another country, Hiking, Camping, Sightseeing, Glass blowing, Playing music, Learning a musical instrument, Boxing, Martial arts, Dirt biking, Drawing, Painting, Sculpting, Birdwatching, Beach walking, Hammock swinging between coconut trees, Burying feet in warm white

Ready. Set. Start!

sandy beaches, Walking the beach at night with romantic partner, Partying, Scuba diving, Boating to other countries, Snorkeling, Reef diving, Ghost hunting , Cave diving, Motor sports, Collecting art, Comic book collections, Learning to fly an airplane, Learning to fly a helicopter, Star gazing, Star counting, Astronomy, Romantic getaways, Playing chess competitively, Fencing, Wrestling, Volleyball, Hotel hopping, Restaurant hopping, Table tennis, Cloud gazing , Golfing, Walking through large fields, Cave explorations, Aeronautics, Shopping, Clothes and wardrobe, Worldwide cultural festivals, Paintball, Worldwide concerts, Mushroom hunting, Sun bathing, Backpacking, Experiences new cultures, Football, Spiritual pilgrimages, Seeing global landmarks, Visiting historical sites, Lake house , City tours, Road tripping in a mobile home, Owning a ranch of horses, Mountain climbing, Storm chasing, Movie making, Inventing, Doing nothing. (just sitting on a chair in the countryside and doing nothing), Reminiscing, Family reunions, Friends reunions, Best friend from long ago reunions, House parties, Visiting events of your mentors.

Ready. Set. Start!

The list is endless because human dreams and desires are endless

Some people are able to do all the things that they love mixed into their schedule.

Reality is that many others have put the majority of their dreams on hold because it's just not possible. The need for money is a limitation, and the need for survival is their reality. The belief is that dreams and desires must be few and in between or completely removed.

Entrepreneurship is rebellion to that belief. Entrepreneurship is hard work, and it takes a lot of time and focus, just like a job. What makes a business different is that it has a much higher possibility to set the Entrepreneur free someday. Free to do all the things he/she loves. Working hard in a job will never completely set an employee free.

The probability and chances are low to none. You may have some time to do a few things but not in perfect freedom. No matter where or what an employee does they must return to the job. Having an own business creates the possibility of setting a person free.

Ready. Set. Start!

That chance, that possibility, that opportunity exists.

Instead of giving up on your dream of doing the things you love. Take the chance. Travel the road of creating and growing your own business. Not because it promises 100% success, but because it is the road that has the opportunity for success.

Having a job doesn't give you that freedom. Having a business gives a person a better chance of reaching that dream. Entrepreneurs do not want to work their whole lives for money. They want to have money work for them.

Too many people are working for money. Entrepreneurs want their money to work hard for them so one day they can do all the things that matter most. The Entrepreneur does this by creating businesses that bring in passive income; money whether the Entrepreneur physically works or not.

SECTION 2

GETTING SET

Ready. Set. Start!

CHAPTER 8
BUSINESS SCHOOL

Many people ask the questions, 'Do I need to go to business school and get a degree to become an Entrepreneur'? The answer is no. Many entrepreneurs did not go to school to learn business.

Some of the best-known Entrepreneurs didn't go to business school or dropped out of college.

1. Bill Gates founder of Microsoft
2. Steve Jobs founder of Apple and Pixar
3. Mark Zuckerberg founder of Facebook
4. Larry Ellison founder of Software development Laboratories (SDL)
5. Jack Dorsey Co-founder of Twitter

Ready. Set. Start!

6. Michael Dell founder of Dell computers
7. Jan Koum founder of WhatsApp

There are countless more examples of Entrepreneurs who didn't finish college and decided to follow their passion and dream. Most people have been trained and molded by the education system to believe that the only way to succeed is through traditional schooling. This is usually people who only understand the limited world of employment.

The Essence and Spirit of Entrepreneurship is unlimited and includes the creation of business through untraveled roads. The best Entrepreneurs have a long history of creating things. It takes a different kind of mentality to do that. Before there is a business an entrepreneur dreams, sacrifices and brings the business to life. He risks failure, ridicule and a loss of security. If he fails, he can be laughed at or go through other social shame. While everyone is waiting to see if he succeeds, he has risked everything to give birth to his new initiative and sacrificed a lot.

Entrepreneurship is about having Courage. Courage to be different, to try different things and to walk down unknown paths. After starting the business, he runs the business for some time, but then he may hire, Business managers. The business managers are important in keeping the business healthy, and this is where business school comes in. Business schools train business managers who are molded in school for one purpose: To work within an existing business. Business managers need an existing business to work in.

Business management is a great and necessary role. I am only trying to point out the differences between the two. Managers may be specialized in one part of the business. Like marketing, business systems, analysis, Human resource, etc. Some managers have generalized training in overseeing broader categories and those who can run an entire business. Business managers belong to the employment section of society. They went to school to get their certificates to get a job. Business schools create workers for the Entrepreneurs business. It is possible for a person who went to business school to be an Entrepreneur. After completing school, he can start his business and run it well. But this is not mandatory. Before you become an entrepreneur, you must spend time learning about all the different business functions. Before you hire someone to fill a gap, you will most likely have to operate there yourself.

An entrepreneur must know a lot about each part and be ready to hire people to take over. It will surprise many people, just how much an entrepreneur can do and function in. Many entrepreneurs are also excellent managers themselves. It is only a matter of choice that he functions in selected roles. As an Entrepreneur you can go ahead and get educated at a college if that's your desire. However, Entrepreneurs do not usually follow conventional educational paths designed for creating an employee mindset. Entrepreneurs take specific and shorter courses that are strategically important.

I recommend taking courses on entrepreneurship from authors who have proven to have a good understanding of the topic. Entrepreneurs learn from other Entrepreneurs. A great way to learn is by working under a successful entrepreneur. This is a great way of learning. Look around you and connect yourself to smart Entrepreneurs.

Learn from your own experiences of attempting, learning, succeeding and failing. You must have your own real-life experiences.

Start small

Start a small business that you can afford to fail in.

If it fails, it will not destroy you financially, and if it succeeds, then you have learned great lessons in the process.

Don't be afraid

Entrepreneurship is about courage.

Be a Reader

Great entrepreneurs are usually avid readers of books and analyzers of the world around them. What books have you read in the recent months? If I ask you to show me all your books, what would I see? Show me your books, and I will tell you your future.

The most valuable material possessions I have is my books. I don't mind leaving my clothes, shoes, car or house behind when migrating, but I value my books. I made it a duty to get every paperback book I had on a digital format and audio book so I can have it on my phone and computer wherever I am.

Get your library in order. Your library must reflect your future self. It's ok to have romantic books and fiction novels. However, you are an Entrepreneur, and most of your books should be on this subject. This separates the serious ones from the amateurs. It is important that you find great examples of Entrepreneurs that you learn from. Read their books, get all their resources and products and watch their journey. Learn as much as you can from them.

The first financial investment to make is an investment in your financial education. Some people put money into advertising or creating a product for their business and no money into their personal development. Your business is an overflow of you, a mirror, and if nothing is being put into you, then what will flow out?

Develop yourself and your mind. Go shopping for some great books and read them.

Mentors

I look for mentors with a deep, meaningful message, whose words and message exude truth.

Ready. Set. Start!

CHAPTER 9

THE DIFFERENT TYPES OF BUSINESSES

Business types

There are different types of business structures and models. Before you enter the world of business, it is a good idea to research all the different kinds of businesses that are out there.

Network marketing

Network marketing is a type of business structure that is popular with people looking for a flexible, part-time business model.

Ready. Set. Start!

Companies like Tupperware, Avon, and Mary Kay Cosmetics are examples of the network marketing model.

Network marketing programs would usually require a low upfront investment. There is a product line offered, and those involved can sell a product directly to friends, family, and other personal contacts. Most network marketing programs also ask participants to recruit other sales representatives. The structure of recruitment creates a 'downline,' and the sales generate income for the seller and those above them. Network marketing systems that focus primarily on recruiting others and not on the selling of the products or services is something to be careful of. A network marketing system in which most of the revenue comes from recruitment may be considered an illegal pyramid scheme.

Watch out for those that are full of hype but doesn't create a high percentage of success for all those involved. Sometimes only those at the top are succeeding based on the recruitment fees. With network marketing, you operate it as your own business. However, you do not own the entire business system or the product.

You sell someone else's product and they will receive the most leverage. Usually it is those who have created the business system that benefits the most. However, it is a good entry point into understanding the world of entrepreneurship.

The training provided, and the mindset taught is great for new entrepreneurs. Do not get involved in it due to hype or over the top high-pressure marketing. Do your own investigation and make intelligent decisions based on facts before investing your money.

Franchises

Franchising is a method of expanding business and distributing goods and services through a licensing relationship. It is a contractual relationship between the Franchisor and Franchisee.

A Franchisor is the legal owner of the business model that grants a license to a third party to conduct business under their trademarks. There is little or no room for making changes and adjustments, the Franchisor determines the operation of the entire business system. The goal of the franchisor is to create a perfect replication of the business model. If you walk into one of their stores, everything you see, experience and buy must be precisely what you would experience in any of the other stores. It is about having uniformity and predictability across the entire franchise system.

The positive thing about franchises is that it is an already proven to be a successful business model. Everyone recognizes the brand, the trademarks, and the products offered. Most of the advertising and branding is done by the franchisor, and the overall value is created by them as well. The person buying the rights to own a franchise is buying into the established success of the business brand.

Franchises are great business opportunities for those who do not want to go through the creation process of a business concept. The already successful business concept has loyal customers and has great momentum. You can find examples of franchises from Fried chicken, pizza outlets, clothes store and any type of market category.

The downside of Franchises is that you are not allowed to get creative. You must do it exactly as the franchisor wants it. If you want to get creative, then do your own thing. Franchises are for people who care more about the financial investment. They invest their money, but all the operational manuals, training, marketing, and designs are controlled by the franchisor. Another disadvantage of franchises is that they are very expensive.

To buy a franchise, you must have a lot of money. Usually the people who buy a franchise are already very rich, have other big businesses and lots of investment money to spare. For people starting off in business, this is not an option as many will have little start-up money to invest. If a person has little initial investment capital, then this may not be the right starting point.

The goal of a new entrepreneur is to start small and grow big over time. Starting off in a network marketing or some other business type may be the best path for them. If you have a lot of money to invest and buying a franchise is right for you, great.

Own business concept

You can start a business based on selected products you have control over. In network marketing, the product is already defined and owned by someone else. In franchises, the product is owned by someone else. You can create a business that is built around your own products or products you can resell. This gives you maximum control and leverage. In time your own product can grow into a network marketing or franchise of its own. The business system around the delivery of the product is also your own. You have the power to handcraft a customized system that will best sell your product.

This is an excellent place to start. It is also wise to research the stories and pathways that successful entrepreneurs took to grow their business.

Legal entities

There are different types of legal business structures.

General Partnership, Limited Partnership, Limited Liability Partnership (LLP), Limited Liability Limited Partnership (LLLP), Corporation, Non-profit, Corporation, Trust,

Joint Venture, Tenants in Common, Municipality, Association, etc.

For the sake of simplicity and for the reasons I hope to achieve in this book, I will focus on the three most common types that I believe relates to most new start-ups.

Sole Proprietorship

A Sole Proprietorship is one individual or married couple in business alone. Sole proprietorships are the most common form of business structure. This type of business is simple to form and operate and may enjoy greater flexibility of management, fewer legal controls, and fewer taxes. However, the business owner is personally liable for all debts incurred by the business. There is very little legal protection for the entrepreneur in this type.

A Limited Liability Company (LLC)

A limited Liability is formed by 1 or more individuals or entities through a special written agreement. The agreement details the organization of the LLC, including provisions for management, assign ability of interests, and distribution of profits and losses. In general, this type of business gives the most protection for the entrepreneur.

The company formed is considered a separate entity from the owner. Where there is litigation and other possible problems, the entrepreneur is better protected.

General Partnership

A General Partnership is composed of 2 or more persons (usually not a married couple) who agree to contribute money, labor, or skill to a business. Each partner shares the profits, losses, and management of the business, and each partner is personally and equally liable for debts of the partnership. Formal terms of the partnership are usually contained in a written partnership agreement. This may be a good option for some. I recommend being careful with this arrangement. The interpersonal problems that arise between partners can be difficult to solve. But there are also many successful Partnership Businesses.

CHAPTER 10

WHAT BUSINESS TO GET INTO

I have been asked by many "what business should I get into?" The answer - I don't know the exact business you should start. I don't know if you should start a coffee shop, a car dealership or an online sales business.

One person may start a car wash business and be miserable because they have no passion for it. They do it for the money and that's not a strong enough reason. Another person may start the same business, a car wash, and absolutely love it. They have a natural passion for it and enjoy each day working on it.

Ready. Set. Start!

I don't know everything about you or your situation, but the person who does know you, and your situation is-YOU! I cannot recommend any specific business, that's something you must decide on your own. What I can do is guide you to make a better-customized choice.

One option is to use the skills you currently possess. If you have a qualification in a subject, you can open a business in that field. If you are an electrician, you can open your own electrical business. If you build websites, you can open a business for building websites.

If you are an oil field technician, start a business in that field. If you are a doctor, start your own private clinic. Use what is in your hands (skill) to create what is in your heart (a business).

This is half of the story.

Some people no longer want to do, what they are currently doing. I spoke with an accountant once. He asked for advice in starting a business. I said, "What about using what you already have. You are a certified accountant, maybe start an accounting firm". I then encouraged him to not be limited by his current skills and to do some soul-searching. He accepted the advice and took the time to find his passion.

Later he returned and admitted the following. The reason he got into accounting was that his father and mother were accountants. He thought that it would be easier to be in that field as they had already paved the way and created some momentum. They laid a foundation, and it was easier to go down the path of least resistance. He also felt pressured into being like them because he didn't want to be a disappointment. His parents and everyone around him never encouraged him to "find himself," instead they encouraged him, very strongly, to be an accountant as well. Ever since he was a small boy, everyone said that he will grow up to be that.

They meant well and just wanted him to have a sense of purpose and a stable job one day. His whole world was surrounded by the life of accountants. He was always encouraged to be like his parents, by people he respected, and he did it like a good boy.

The only thing is, his real self wasn't in love with it. He had the skills, the certifications, and

Ready. Set. Start!

the know-how, but it was mainly for job security.

In his soul-searching he knew he loved online marketing. He is passionate about it and loves it, so he decided to develop a new skill. He proceeded to learn more about online marketing. This time, it was about Him and who he truly was. Some of the people around him were confused as to why he would try something new, and a few even tried to indirectly discourage his new venture. He persevered and pursued a business dream in online marketing. Today he is doing very well and doesn't have to live the rest of his life living everyone else's dream for him. Therefore, I advise people: When searching for a type of business to get into, do something you love, first.

If it is a skill you currently have, then great.

If what you love is a new skill to be learned, then start.

It's never too late to learn new things.

There are personalities testing available online. Check the skills you currently have and those skills you want to have. However, do not be limited to the skills you currently have.

Ready. Set. Start!

Turn what is in your heart (passion) into what is in your hand (skill) into what is in your heart (dreams, business) into what is in your heart (freedom)

Many people value being known for having one skill. This is especially true in the world of employment. The more specialized you are, the more employable you are. Entrepreneurs don't want to be pinned down to one skill. They cannot afford to have one skill, so they are ready to learn a new skill at any time.

When an entrepreneur starts down a new road, some may find it hard to understand because they are infatuated with the last road. After some time, when they see results, they slowly come around. A real-life lesson to be learned here is that, in the beginning, an entrepreneur is usually alone in his dream. Once he begins to succeed, the whole world magically remembers who he is.

When a gladiator stands in the arena, half of the stadium is waiting to see him win, the other half is waiting to see him lose.

You cannot live for the approval of the crowd, you must live for your dream. Do not dislike the half who doesn't support you, because you will only become the monster you claim to be fighting against.

The monster of hatred, unforgiveness, negativity, and anger. Do good to those who dislike you and help everyone rise.

Be the one who is above it all. Your dream will one day help many people, maybe even those who didn't believe. I certainly hope so. Let's make the world a more positive place.

CHAPTER 11

MARKETS

A Market is where there is a demand and a supply. People want things (a demand), and a supply (products and service) is created to meet it.

Demands are based on human wants, needs, and desires. The demand is what drives markets. As you prepare to drive down a road (enter a market) and start a business, remember this: Some markets are dead-end streets. If a person doesn't watch markets, they will become a victim of the market's factors.

I discussed this topic throughout the book that you must lift your eyes and look at the global picture. It's not enough to look at what's happening in your neighborhood, country or region of the world. If you are involved in vehicles, you belong to the automotive industry- worldwide. If you are into graphic design, you belong to the Creative design industry- worldwide. If you are into printing magazines, you are in the publishing industry- worldwide.

This may sound like a no-brainer, but many people are operating without knowing the industry they are in. This is important to know so you can track the behavior and life expectancy of your industry.

Many industries are closing.

Every market has a life expectancy: It has time to be born and a time to die. Many industries may look strong now but in 10 years will be gone. The wave of unemployment and shutdowns may not have hit your hometown yet, but there may be a tsunami on the way.

Look at the demand of the market for your industry. Does enough people want what you offer? When Judging markets look at the Global Financial situation. For example. If you are in the oil and gas industry, what are the global financial realities? I live in a country that wants to have fossil-free energy in one generation. That means no more reliance on the traditional fuels we have today.

Many nations want to stop buying the commonly used fuels in the future and are turning to Renewable energy sources. It may take years to accomplish, but the ship has already started changing its course.

Many malls and shopping centers are closing as more products and services are being offered online. There may have been an entrepreneur who spent millions of dollars on his new mall, only to realize it is not as profitable as projected. These online businesses have replaced many 'cannot fail, super giants' in the physical world.

Some markets are expected to have future growth. Do your own research on markets that are doing well and have a good outlook for the future. After you have researched it yourself, be motivated by intelligence and not greed. Get involved only in markets that are doing well and show great promise for the future.

Don't blindly chase every new trend. Think and make sure that what you are getting into has value to offer and lasting power.

Ready. Set. Start!

You want to be a part of the future, not the past. There are past ways of thinking, that is dead, and some people try their best to keep it alive. Trying to keep a market alive on artificial life support, through hard work, is not ideal. Imagine there is a phone company that is selling corded phones. It has a long wire that connects to the wall. The phone has large physical buttons to dial.

The company is spending millions of dollars on the product and on marketing hoping to keep that market alive. That time has passed. That is an example of investing money into something that people no longer want. When something is working and will continue to do so, never give up. When something is dead or not coming back, its ok to give up, in that case. You must know when it's time to give up.

I heard a legend of the Titanic. I cannot confirm if it's true. The Legend says that when the boat first hit the iceberg, no human person on the ship was in a panic to leave. However, all the rats and little animals knew by instinct that there was trouble. They all started looking for a way out of the boat, first. They had foresight and instinct of the danger.

Ready. Set. Start!

Unfortunately, many intelligent humans didn't see the need to evacuate the doomed ship in time. Only later, when the trouble was more evident, did people try to evacuate.

Sometimes when the ship is sinking, the rats jump out first. Stay alert. Look at the most intelligent people and their movements. They are usually following something. If they are jumping out of trends and markets, ask yourself why. However, keep your own eyes on the trends and make decisions that you believe is best. Don't blindly follow what others are doing, only take it as something to consider.

There are markets yet to be created. I was used to having a cell phone with a tiny pixelated screen and little physical knobs. I would try to type on them, with much difficulty. Steve Jobs created a brand-new product. The iPhone. It had no letters and number pad. It was a touch screen, and it was smart. It was the birth of a new smartphone. Steve Jobs created an entirely new market and category. Now, everyone can hardly imagine a time without a smartphone. This is what some Entrepreneurs do. They make and create new markets. They invent new products and develop new initiatives.

Ready. Set. Start!

As an entrepreneur, you do not have to be limited to doing something that already exists or is trending. You can make the new trend. It was entrepreneurs that created things like Facebook, Instagram, Twitter, Uber, the smartphone, the computer, Software, apps, etc. Most innovations and breakthroughs, in history, were introduced to the market by Entrepreneurs. Right now, people are living in an apartment building. They work hard and pay their rent. Nothing is wrong with this. We all need a roof over our heads. Before there was an apartment building, an entrepreneur, saved, dreamed, budgeted, planned, hired construction crews and worked diligently for a long time to create that apartment complex.

The result of that hard work is many people being able to have a place to live. Some renters in the apartment complex may not care about the creation process, they may care about the creation: The roof over their head. It was Entrepreneurship that created the apartment building.

The spirit of Entrepreneurship led to the creation of something valuable. If the renter also falls in love with Entrepreneurship, one day he can become an apartment building

Ready. Set. Start!

owner as well. Take your eyes off the creation and start looking towards examples of creators. Don't just look at your iPhone's screen and scroll, think about the creator of the iPhone. What drove him to create. What were his motivations and the things he knew?

When scrolling through Facebook or Instagram, don't only care about the creation. Ask yourself what led to the creation of these things. When you walk into a coffee shop, don't just enjoy a cup of coffee. Ask yourself questions as to how this coffee shop got started and is being run. Consumers focus on getting the products, Entrepreneurs focus on the creative processes. Entrepreneurs create the things that make our world go around. Before the car was invented, everyone was doing fine riding horses and trains everywhere. It took an entrepreneur to push the design, dream, and introduction of the new product to the world.

Now many people have cars. Before the car was invented, everyone was comfortable and had settled in their known way of life. People do not always understand that life can be better, and they need someone to show them that it can be better. Entrepreneurs love to create. The jobs that people will have in the future are being created by the entrepreneurs of today.

Entrepreneurs bring about change

I remember when my wife, Jhessicka and I had a real estate company, I was contacted by an owner of a property. She was very frustrated, confused and tired. She had a property that was in a good location but was in terrible condition. For many years she tried to do something with that property, but it seemed impossible. She was ready to give up. We decided to help, mainly because of the challenge. The place was dilapidated, dark, full of graffiti and an eyesore. There were illegal and homeless occupants living in it who were on drugs. Whenever the owner or others passed by the property, they were threatened with violence. There was no functioning toilet, so the placed smelled and looked bad. There was no electricity, and it was filled with birds and other wild animals, cohabitating with the people. We initiated several steps to get the place improved and to create some change. The police got involved in helping humanely relocate the illegal inhabitants to a better facility (a homeless shelter) where they could be better cared for. We worked on it for some months. I remember one night, my wife and I were driving on a busy, well-known road and to my right, there was a fully functional, beautiful and occupied restaurant. It looked amazing, clean and modern. We only smiled to each other as we drove by, remembering that it was once a community shame.

This is what Entrepreneurs do, they love to bring about positive change. If you love to see things change for the better and you are driven to do something about it, you have the Entrepreneurial spirit. Use that desire, to create a business, that not only makes money but brings about change.

CHAPTER 12

THE BUSINESS PLAN

If you plan your business well, it will save you a lot of damage control later. It's like building a house. When it is completed, the walls are new, the paint is fresh, and it looks and smells great.

Two weeks later you read a great book and decide to upgrade and improve on the house. You have learned some new things that can make your home so much better. Some of the enhancements can be easily done whereas some of the changes may be deep and foundational. You grab the sledgehammer and start breaking down walls and windows. If you knew what was needed earlier, you wouldn't have to pay for an expensive renovation.

Ready. Set. Start!

A business is like a tree. Before there is a tree, there is a seed. The type of tree is determined by the type of seed planted.

If it's an apple seed, it will create an apple tree.

If it's a mango seed, it will create a mango tree.

The seed affects what the outcome is.

A business plan is like a seed. If a business is planned and designed well, it has a better chance of growing into a success. Before anyone builds a house, they must first have a plan. A plan that is well thought out, written out and even drawn out.

A Blueprint

This is a physical drawing that you can hold in your hands and instantly see the drawn plans of each system of the house and how they will work together. The intention is to have all the parts, working together to achieve one meaningful goal. The Entrepreneur must have a Business plan, a business' version of a blueprint. It must contain all the systems that a business needs to be healthy.

The Entrepreneur creates a business plan before there is a business. Before there is anything tangible or evident, the Entrepreneur spends time planning the business. A lot of the work is done before there is a business. The dreaming and planning stages are long and intensive.

The Entrepreneur needs to be able to see the big picture at any time and see how the different systems work together to form a whole. If your business is already up and running, but you didn't put a lot into planning it, then go ahead and write up a business plan. It will help you organize your ideas and give you a much clearer understanding of your business. Start drawing up plans. Have the power to see what's going on and to be able to address the health of the system.

There are two types of business plans

The first one is for your eyes only. In this plan, you have all the details of your business and the inner workings of the entire structure. This is a very large and detailed plan. If people see this, their mind may drift, they may get bored, and they will lose concentration. This one is not designed for public viewing, it's more for your own motivation and understanding of the business. Investors and partners do not have the time to read through a document of hundreds of pages long.

The second one is a shorter version that is a summary of the first business plan. This plan is for potential investors and partners to read and gives you a general overview of your business. This one is designed for others to view because it gives summaries of large categories.

Making a business plan has advantages. It keeps the business on track towards goals and objectives. It also helps you communicate your plan to those who may be willing to invest in the business. You will need to have an open mind. When you start researching the many parts of your business plan, reality will set in. The reality of the competition, costs, and the skills required will be an eye-opener.

Be flexible.

The Big Why

The first part of your business plan must be the Big Why? The Purposes and reasons for starting the business. This includes your visions and goal and must come first in the plan.

Why does your business exist?

What is your vision statement?

What is your mission statement?

What are your lists of goals?

Where do you want your business to be in the future?

What is the short-term, mid-term and long-term dreams for your business? What is the problem that the business is a solution for? Don't rush this part. Take the time to write down your answers to these questions. This is your foundation and must be laid well.

Market Research

Define your target

Who are you targeting?

Is it adults, children, men, women, the rich, the middle class? Do research to understand who these people are, how they think and why they would want to interact with your product. What is the target age of your audience? What are their likes, dislikes, interests, and preferences? It makes no sense creating a product that doesn't fit your target audience.

Learn as much as possible about your target. You desire to create something of value that supplies a solution to a need that they have. If you do not understand what they need and want, you may be missing the bullseye. Find resources that help you understand your audience. Find censuses, demographic analysis, and other market research tools.

Players on the Field

This is commonly known as Competition research. There are people out there making products and services that people want. As a business owner, you are entering this sphere. You need to know who the players in the game are. What makes them great or not great. You can learn from the ones who have great influence and success. Gather information on them and see what type of system they are using.

The ones who are failing can be also be learned from. You can learn what not to do. Knowing what doesn't work is vital

Ready. Set. Start!

information. Whatever field of business you are entering, find those who are already in it and see what they are doing. If you make soft drinks, then go out to the store and buy all the soft drinks you can find.

Taste them all.

Watch the packaging.

Look at the bottle, the shape, and the size.

Look at the marketing for the drink in the store. Was there an accompanying sign at the point of sale? Look at their advertising on social media and on TV etc. Research how they produce their products and what factory equipment they use. The goal is not to reproduce a copy of what they have. The goal is to understand the wheel that has already been invented. You can be better informed for when you create your own customized, unique wheel.

Other people will see you as their competition and put all your products, services and processes under the microscope to learn what to be and not to be. When analyzing the competition ask some of these questions.

What are the products and services being offered?

Ready. Set. Start!

What is the pricing and costs?

How many customers do they have?

What is their quality overall?

How does their product and service make people feel?

How is their branding and image?

What makes them special from others in their field? How are the workers? Are they happy or seem depressed? Create a chart to make everything visually understandable. You can create a field for pricing and add the different prices. For example, if one competitor has a 500ml soda for $2 and another competitor has the same 500ml soda type for $3 write it down so you can see the price variances.

This will help you know how to place yourself and your pricing when you come to market. If your 500 ml soda is $10, that shows that your competition research on pricing was faulty. As someone new entering a market dominated by big names and multimillion-dollar budgets in advertising, you must be realistic in your entry pricing, to be competitive in the market.

Ready. Set. Start!

Product

What are you offering your customers?

If it is a product, write a plan on how to create your product. The product must go through these stages

Product concept

This is coming up with what you want to sell. You may have a list of options and then finally decide on one.

Product research

After you have decided what you want to make, you must now find out how to make it and all the other information needed

Product design

This is the design phase. For example, if you decided that the product is a T-shirt, you need to create the designs for the t-shirt. What is the Shape, size, color, print, body fit, etc? Who will be doing the designs? If you are not qualified yourself to do the design, you will need to hire a professional.

Product manufacture

After you have the designs, you can send it into production. What are all the things needed to create the product? Who will be doing the manufacturing? Do you need to get manufacturing equipment yourself? Are you going to outsource the manufacturing process to specialists?

Product placement

Where are customers going to interact with your product? How and where can they get it? If you are selling T-shirts. Where can your customers get them? Is it on a website? Is it in a brick and mortar store?

Product delivery

How is it delivered to customers? What are all the considerations of delivering the product? Is delivery supplied by yourself or by another company? I also call it Distribution.

Marketing

Marketing is a huge Category.

Marketing alone can fill many books. Marketing is about getting your message out and getting the right people to know what you offer.

Ready. Set. Start!

Branding

This is the desired long-term image of your company and products, in the minds of people. It is a culmination of all the experiences, thoughts and perceptions of what you are. It is the equivalent of the reputation of a person. Branding must be done by design and with creative thought. There are branding specialists can give you counsel and advice.

Advertising

Advertising is a means of communication with the users of a product or service. Advertisements are messages paid for by those who send them and are intended to inform or influence people who receive them, as defined by the Advertising Association of the UK. People are very busy, distracted and constantly bombarded by information and advertising. How do you create an advertisement that cuts through the noise? The advertisement is launched out to the customers to get their attention, to introduce yourself and to encourage the buy-in of your products.

Ready. Set. Start!

Online marketing

This is a science. You need to use all the online tools available to you. Social media- Facebook, Instagram, YouTube, etc.

Search engine Optimization

This is the process of getting traffic from search engine results.

Websites

Most people have a website for their business. All the platforms must work together as a cohesive whole to funnel and channel your marketing and sales.

Offline Marketing

This is a category of marketing that includes the physical world. Some call it traditional marketing. If your t-shirt business is based online and the advertising is done on the web, you may also want to advertise through conventional means. Newspaper, magazine, radio, television, banner and signage etc. Locations will include public places, malls, roadway signage, etc.

I will not recommend one over the other. Do whatever works and is getting results for your product. However, I personally prefer to concentrate my marketing efforts online.

LEGAL

I recommend hiring a lawyer for legal advice and services. Choose the type of legal entity you will be functioning as. Sole proprietorship, Limited Liability, Partnership, etc. I described earlier the different types of businesses, choose one.

Every country has its own rules and processes for legally registering a business. I recommend finding a good lawyer who can help you with the legal setting up process. They do not have to be fulltime on your team, just paid for their consultation hours, etc. Find good lawyers who specialize in business law. Some lawyers are specialists in different types of law practices. For example, litigation, family and marriage, Real Estate, etc. I prefer to find a lawyer who specializes in business matters. The process should include name registration and business type registration.

Ready. Set. Start!

FINANCIAL

Create Financial projections.

Financial projections are speculations and forecasts, in anticipation of what things may cost. The Financial projections must include how the business will generate income, where money will be spent, what assets and liabilities the business will have. For expenses, write a comprehensive list of cost that will be involved. Remember that every part of your business involves costs.

You will need a comprehensive financial plan that includes information on setting up a bank account and tax information. Be sure to get the necessary advice. The Financial structure includes many things that must be understood and put in place. Search for a financial system model and get professional help from an accountant.

A budget for the Product

What will it cost to go through the entire process of creating your product. Some costs to write-down-Product design. Creating the designs of your product will require very specialized services. If you are designing a car for example. The costs of designing that product will include the work of engineers, artists, computer aided drawings and many other specialities.

There will be the need for testing and experimentation in developing the product. The car may have to pass certain quality tests before it is approved. Define clearly what your product is and list all costs involved.

Every other part of your business will incur costs

Create a budget for each section of the business

Legal work

Marketing

Consultants/freelancers etc.

Include all costs for salaries and whatever else is needed. After you have calculated all the projected costs for each section, make one final total amount. This will be considered your start-up costs.

More advice on the business plan. Keep every chapter brief and concise. If it is too long, it may discourage others from reading it. Investors, partners, and others that you hope to share it with will appreciate it.

Ready. Set. Start!

Believe in yourself

It may be your first time creating a business plan. You may feel intimidated or inexperienced but keep pushing forward. Everyone in business had a starting point as well. Give it your best shot and don't forget to research examples of business plans that work. If you think its best to get professional help, you can hire a specialist who can assist in the creation of business plans. Work with them to get your vision documented.

The Executive Summary

This is an overview of the entire plan.

People reading it can jump around the document and find specific chapters and topics. It's like a table of contents for a book.

SECTION 3

GETTING STARTED

CHAPTER 13

CONFIDENCE

Confidence is the feeling or belief that one can have faith in or rely on someone or something. Confidence is about having trust in someone or something. Confidence takes time to be built. As you are getting ready to start a business people must be able to trust you and believe in you. Before you try to get others to Believe in you first work on believing in yourself.

Self-confidence

Ready. Set. Start!

Self-confidence is one of the most critical parts of Entrepreneurship. Self-confidence is a magnetic force and is a major part of the makeup of an entrepreneur. I'm not talking about arrogance, bullying, pride or being obnoxious. I'm talking about being politely and respectfully assured of yourself.

What creates self-confidence? If someone puts me in Russia and tells me to speak Russian to everyone around, I will not have the confidence to do it. This is because I don't know Russian, If someone places me on a baseball field and puts a bat in my hand, I will not have the confidence to play the game. I don't know anything about it. I don't know the rules. If someone asks me about entrepreneurship, I can confidently speak about it because I believe and have faith in my knowledge of the subject.

Confidence is a result of having Know-how. Everyone has things that they are confident and not confident about. What decides between the two is what you have invested time and energy in. If you spend time and energy on Entrepreneurship, your confidence in that topic will rise. Confidence is important. No one wants to follow a leader

Ready. Set. Start!

who has a lot of self-doubts and a lack of confidence. A lack of conviction and belief never make a good leader. Your business is borrowing your confidence. People will have confidence in your business if you are confident in it

Your business is taking all its confidence from you and is acting like a sponge. Whatever you are giving off, your business will soak up. You must exude confidence. You must have confidence in the type of business you are involved in. I have had many people try to get me involved in a business idea. I didn't do it because I didn't feel confident about the type of business.

I am confident in what I truly believe in. Having self-confidence is important because you are selling yourself. You are selling your dreams. You are selling your product. You need to have a genuine belief in these things. Before you can believe in a dream, a product or a business, you must first believe in yourself.

Believe in You. Believe in your abilities. Believe in your knowledge. Believe that you can be successful. Many see confidence as having pride. Being boastful or a brag. This can be true of some people, but Confidence is a vital quality to have. It is a must-have. Confidence is vital I have seen leaders and people in business who lacked confidence in themselves. They always see themselves as a victim. There always seem to be some enemy after them. They are extremely enemy focused. They are always talking about giving up, quitting and how depressed they are. They portray themselves as the whole world being against them, and how many people do not like them. They prefer to influence people through self-pity and being a victim. They may attract others like that, but not true winners. I don't want to follow people like that, do you?

There is not a single person who doesn't struggle with low confidence in themselves at times. There will be moments in life where we will encounter self-doubt. When we experience failure and defeat, our self-confidence is deeply hurt. This must be a temporary occasion, not a permanent state of being. You must get back up and get your confidence back. Entrepreneurship is about this battle of retaining self-confidence through great troubles. If you are struggling with self-confidence, work hard on improving it. Get help and research ways of boosting your self-confidence. If the problem is very serious, consider speaking with a counselor or a professional. Do not let low self-esteem and a low self-image keep you in prison.

Self-confidence comes from the truth. The truth of who you really are on the inside. People will have confidence in things that are real and true. When someone is speaking about something that they believe in, there is a difference in their voice and body language. They are more confident. This is because they are telling the truth. Now, I know people who lie and steal and cheat their way into things and still manage to put on a confident front. They are fakes and masters of putting on a good show. The problem with this is that they are still faked. Their life is just a show. Your goal is to be real. To be the real deal.

Develop your Skills

The more you read books and research Entrepreneurship, the more you really develop and grow. Taking the time to "take a long way" and not "the shortcuts" is the way to be real. You must really know your stuff. Get the right books and make no excuses, read them. Page by page, word by word. Try to understand the essence of what is being communicated

Self-confidence can be developed and built. Anyone can become a more confident person.

1. Stop and remember where you came from. You have past victories and successes, let that inspire you.

2. Take control of your mind. Don't let your emotions and self- talk be negative and defeating.

3. Take control of your sphere. Find ways to be surrounded by a positive atmosphere. Remove yourself from negative things.

4. Get help. Find people you can talk to and will not judge you People that you can honestly share your feelings with. Get counsel and advise on how to boost your confidence

Sell confidence

Self-confidence creates Sell confidence. I have never heard this saying before. I didn't borrow it from someone. I was in deep thought about this subject of why self-confidence is important. I am always wary of people who quote others but never have a good original quote. Sayings must be generated from a deep part of who you truly are.

If someone gives me a product that I do not understand and tell me to go sell it, I won't be able to do so with confidence. Some people may be able to because they are good actors. But I'm not wired like that. I am not confident in putting on a show. Confidence for me must be raw, real and full of truth. I have had people ask me to follow them into certain things. I couldn't do it with a clear conscience and refused. I didn't believe that the values they stood for were truly what I believed in. I am confident about things I know. I am confident about the things I am sure of

Selling

Selling is one of the most important skills of an entrepreneur. A person can be an Actor seller. A person can be a Believer Seller. Selling is the transfer of Confidence. You cannot transfer what you do not have. You can only transfer what you do have. You can go to all the sales training and sales schools if you don't

Ready. Set. Start!

have confidence you cannot truly sell. Sell confidence comes from self-confidence.

Have confidence in yourself

Have confidence in your business

Have confidence in your message

Have confidence in your product

Have confidence in your dreams

Have confidence in your continual success

Have confidence in your marketability

I have created things in the past, and when it was time to market it, I was motivated and on fire to sell it. I have created other things and when it was time to market it, I just couldn't. I didn't believe it was at the quality it should be at. I shut down the program and didn't advertise it.

To truly sell something, you must believe in it. To sell your vision and dreams, you must believe in your vision and dreams. I am confident in selling this book because I believe in the message and the value it will give to people. I am dreaming of helping many thousands of people through this book. I believe that the information here, works and will change people's lives. If I didn't believe in this book, I will be unsure about it and never advertise it. I believe in its value and ability to change people, for the better. I will confidently sell it and will search for those who also believe in it and are willing to get it in everyone's hands. You must have that attitude towards your products.

Think about what you offer and check your confidence level concerning it. If what you offer is a high quality, value-enhancing product. GO for it! If it is not a good product. Find something better. Working on building knowledge and experiences in life gives the confidence to sell. Work on your knowledge and abilities. Work on developing the value of what you create. Let what you do and create truly have the power to impact people. Don't get into business primarily for money. Don't get into selling firstly for the profit or other perceived benefits. Let the motivation be- "adding real value to people" and let the money be a bonus. Imagine you are the customer. Do you want that product being sold? Will you buy it yourself? Is it going to add value to your life?

Ready. Set. Start!

Creating public confidence

An entrepreneur hoping to enter the marketplace will need to develop public confidence. This is when the people in public can trust you. One way of gaining this trust is to get wins under your belt. Start a project and win at it. When people see this, a little more confidence is built. Continue going through a series of wins and one success at a time will lead to a higher level of public confidence. You must also maintain integrity and good character.

Creating customer confidence

Everything that applies to public confidence applies to customer confidence. The customers come from the public space and will be influenced by that; however, customers are not the same as the public. The public is the bystanders that watch from a distance, whereas the customers are those who have decided to take it one step further. They have chosen to buy your product or service, and that means they deserve respect for taking that step.

Ready. Set. Start!

An entrepreneur must work on gaining and maintaining customer confidence in his business, products, and services.

How? Deliver. When you make a promise, deliver on that promise. Breaking promises on delivery is a no-no.

Time-

Keep appointments, meetings, and promises about showing up. Missing appointments and being late is dishonesty, in my book. You promised to be there and to be on time. No one is perfect, and there will be times of unexpected delays, etc. This should not be the norm, but an occasional event. If you are running late due to an emergency, then maintain good communication to those waiting. Keep your promise, and you will keep the confidence of others.

Quality –

Keep your products and service at High quality.

Consistency-

You must be consistent in delivering on your word. People don't watch the one-off good service, they watch the whole story. Your business is a story on a timeline, and it's in full

Ready. Set. Start!

view of the customers. Always think of long-term effect, not just the short term.

CHAPTER 14

STEREOTYPES

There is good and bad in every sector of Society. In everything in the world, wherever there are people, they will be positive things and negative things. This applies to the world of entrepreneurship as well. Some entrepreneurs have done a great job and have set a marvelous example. They show us that Entrepreneurship is a noble and fulfilling way of life. We need more of these people to be showcased and used as examples. Unfortunately, some entrepreneurs went upstream and muddied the waters, and some downstream can be negatively affected by it. Their actions have made it more difficult for good entrepreneurs to function.

Ready. Set. Start!

One reason people don't start their business is because they are afraid of the negative stereotypes attached to Entrepreneurship. They are afraid of people seeing them in a negative light. This fear is crippling to some, and the 'would-be Entrepreneurs' are intimidated out of the idea. Identify the stereotypes so that you can overcome them.

Negative Stereotypes

1. Entrepreneurs are Materialistic

Many people believe that being an entrepreneur means being a materialistic person. It doesn't help when some people post pictures of themselves with handfuls of cash, fanning themselves with the cash or swimming in it. It's raining money in their golden apartment, and they have all the fanciest, shiniest stuff. They Promote themselves with private jets, large yachts, and sports cars. These people minimize the true essence of Entrepreneurship. They reduce is to material things and to an image that is not helpful. This may attract a shallow few, but it's a turn off for most, myself included. If you are a person with private jets, sports cars and all the flashy things, good for you. Nothing is wrong with these things. What I have a problem with is when people sell the idea that "This is mainly what entrepreneurship is about." They make it the front and center of the reason for entrepreneurship, and I disagree with that.

I believe that the essence of entrepreneurship is not about material things, but about solving problems. It's about adding value to the lives of people. Helping people out of the unfavorable situations they are in. It's about accomplishing your dreams and doing it with a level of humility. Its ok to talk about your success so others can understand your story and experiences, but it's not helpful to make it mostly about the material things. This is my opinion.

2. Entrepreneurs are greedy

This stereotype is that they are heartless people who are just in it for money and will get it at any cost. This is false. There are many good-hearted and generous Entrepreneurs in the world. At the heart and soul of

Ready. Set. Start!

Entrepreneurship is the desire to help people and to give generously. Many of the best Entrepreneurs around the world are very generous with their money and time. They volunteer at non-profit organizations, they donate to charities and are philanthropists. They initiative drives to build schools, hospitals and help the needy and the poor. They donate to causes that solve major world problems and help create cures for diseases etc. They also create jobs and opportunities for people to be able to have meaningful employment and a financial foundation.

The image of Scrooge doesn't help. We all know the Christmas story of the very greedy and stingy Scrooge. Before he was transformed into a good-hearted person, he typified the greedy business person stereotype. He didn't share, he was self-centered, greedy and hoarded all his success. Money is only an amplifier and a mirror of the person using it. If a person is greedy, money will only reflect that. If the person is generous, money will reflect that. Money is not the problem, it's the condition of the heart of a person, that is a potential problem. Some people are afraid to admit to their friends and family that they are into a network marketing business because they are afraid of appearing greedy.

The stereotype is intimidating. I heard this advice from a social media expert. She said, "Don't let people around you know that you have a business, or that you are into network marketing, and don't talk about it on your social media". I disagree. You must be free to talk about your business. This is how people will know what you offer and believe in. If someone is completely unhappy about you being in business, then you need to create a circle of people who better understand your dreams and where you are headed.

You need to be surrounded by people who are like minded and understand where you are headed in life. This stereotype is discouraging too many people from getting into business and is pressuring people to play it safe in their job, where everyone will like them.

3. They are high-pressure salespeople

Many people do not become an entrepreneur because they are afraid that others will think that they are high pressure, fast-talking salesperson. Some high-pressure salespeople have given the world of business a bad name.

The high-pressure person only cares about getting a sale at all cost. All entrepreneurs must be able to sell. If you cannot sell, you cannot be in business. However, communicating to people what you offer and how it can help them must be done in a way that encourages buying without manipulation. You must also sell with a correct motive, which is to genuinely help people. If the motive is money only, that is not right. Love people and use things.

You must communicate what you offer to people, the benefits and advantages that they could enjoy. People must then see for themselves that they can benefit from what you offer.

The goal should be High positive influence selling. Not high pressure and manipulation. I mentioned the advice I heard from the expert; not to let anyone around you and on your social media know that you have a business. This person also mentioned that the reason they recommend this is because "you don't want to appear to be a high-pressure salesman." Think about that. A new entrepreneur is being told not to present their business to people because of the fear of this one stereotype. That stereotype is so scary to some people that they are willing to pretend to not be in business at all.

In starting your own business, you must not be afraid of what people think and the stereotypes. If you are too scared of it, you may not get into business. My Advice: Get into business, tell people what you offer and sell, then show everyone around that a person can succeed without being a high pressure, manipulative salesman. We can all help to break the negative stereotype. Let your Success in business be an example to future generations of Entrepreneurship done right. Let everyone see that through respect, honor, integrity, morality, humility, dignity, influence and passion a person can be successful.

Everything in life has stereotypes, yet people rise above them and become successful, proving the stereotypes wrong. Be courageous, brave and step out to reach for your dreams.

CHAPTER 15

STARTING

There are specific reasons why people don't start their business. Let us identify some of these reasons so we can take the necessary steps to remove them.

1. Fear

The number one reason people do not start their own business is Fear. More people have lived below their potential, because of fear, than any other reason.

Here are some common fears

The fear of Failure

The fear of What others may think

The fear of Looking bad

The fear of Embarrassing themselves

The fear of Being misunderstood

Ready. Set. Start!

The fear of Being Stereotyped

2. Not knowing enough

One reason people do not start their business is the Lack of knowledge. It is important to be always learning and increasing in knowledge. This can keep you humble and open to learning. You should keep researching and learning what is needed to start your business.

However, if left unchecked, this can turn into a perpetual cycle called: Analysis Paralysis. This is where a person is continually learning without any accompanying action. They learn, learn some more and then learn even more and never do anything about what they have learned, because they want to learn some more first.

Overcome this obstacle. Your objective is to remove all the reasons for not starting your business. Speed up the process of learning and if you believe that you have more to learn, get the information you need, faster.

Do more research, faster. Sacrifice watching TV, going out to party and other activities for a while. Use the time instead to read, learn and research. Change your entire life schedule and create the extra time needed to read.

Manufacture the time. Sleep later at night and wake earlier in the morning if you must. Stop making the lack of knowledge an excuse. Some people never get into business because they always feel like they don't know enough. This can go on forever. Many tombstones have the invisible words engraved, I never tried because I didn't think I knew enough to start. Don't get stuck in this mental quicksand. Create an organized reading, studying, researching and planning schedule. Most importantly – START!!!

I can find millions of talkers, I usually find fewer doers. Be someone who takes Action.

3. Too Busy

Some people believe that they are too busy. Busyness is having a lot of activity. Some people pride themselves in being busy. They wear it as a badge of honor. Having a lot of activity alone is not impressive to me and is not the key to success. Having activity around what truly matters is what leads to success. Search

Ready. Set. Start!

your calendar and activities and re-prioritize all your activities. The truth is, people are not truly busy, they only prioritize what's important to them. If you say that starting your business is a priority, then let your calendar show it.

Some people make busyness an excuse. They lack the self-discipline to do what matters. They hide behind the excuse of busyness, but it's a front. They make themselves feel busy to justify their fear of starting. They say, 'look at my schedule, I'm very busy, that's why I can't start my business.'

Most times, this is a mask to hide the fear.

We have two choices.

Choose Fear and Fail.

Choose Courage and Succeed.

Fear is not about the way you feel. We all feel fear.

Fear is about making a choice to freeze.

Courage is not about never feeling afraid. Courage is about choosing to move forward despite negative feelings.

Courage or Fear -Choose one.

I want you to choose Courage.

Ready. Set. Start!

I believe the person reading this book is Courageous and capable.

4. Being Unprepared

Get yourself prepared.

I shared the details of creating a business plan and other steps needed to be taken. Go through the steps and get ready.

5. Naivety

Every successful person has fallen and gotten back up many times. In your journey, you will have moments of success and moments of learning the hard way. This is part of the process to be realistic in understanding that the road will not be a straight line, but curvy and includes mountains and valleys. Be determined and committed to the process and don't be afraid to go through some setbacks and temporary failures. Think about the long-term vision and dream.

6. Feeling Satisfied

This is a dangerous reason for why people don't start. They may have a decent job, salary and a socially acceptable "average life." They feel emotionally safe in their current career, safe in their accomplishments and are satisfied. If your goal is to start your own business, being satisfied where you are right now is a dangerous thing. It's like being put to sleep. When people are ready to undergo a major surgery, the medical professionals would usually give the patient special medication that will put them to sleep. The patient does not fall asleep because of natural tiredness, it's a sleep due to the influence of the drug. If you know deep down that Entrepreneurship is for you but feel satisfied with your life and with your job, be careful, you may be under the influence of a 'drug.'

The drug of mediocrity. The drug of being satisfied with where you are at. If you need to climb a mountain, run a race or operate heavy machinery, you know that you cannot be using sleep inducing medication. The same is true for Entrepreneurship. Do not put yourself to sleep by settling for just ok. Your goal should be excellence and striving for higher levels of accomplishment.

In the context of stepping out into your own, do not let being satisfied put you to sleep. A common experience we go through is

Ready. Set. Start!

when trying to wake up early in the morning, we hear the alarm, but say to ourselves, "just 5 more minutes." Awaking yourself from a deep sleep can be tough so be ready for a fight. You must shake off the sleep of settling and being satisfied.

7. Not set launching date

This is a major point to remember. You must set a launch date and stick to it.

The Day of Commitment

I recommend having a specific day on your calendar called "the day of commitment." Create a personal document that is like a contract to yourself. Write the reasons for starting the business and a promise to start it. On that day you will sign and commit to the promise of starting your business. After signing the document, keep it somewhere visible. You may choose to have a few close friends, or your spouse hold you accountable to it.

The document states that you have decided to start your own business, without making any more excuses.From the date of your signing, you now have 9 months to start your business.

Launch Date

Create a launch date of within 9 months of your signing.If you can launch earlier, then great, however, nine months is my recommended limit.If you spread it out over too long a time frame, it will lack focus, urgency, and momentum.The next nine months must be focused and concentrated.People will learn whether to trust you or not based on your ability to deliver on your launch date promises.Make your launch date Public and consider it a promise, then keep your promise (launch it).Taking this important step is worth it.All the hard work, sacrifice, and courage of getting started has the potential to pay off greatly.Pay the price now for a better tomorrow.Start small and grow over time.

Overcoming all the obstacles of fears and personal doubt is what will take you to success.Organize, plan and execute your plan.Every successful entrepreneur has gone through these steps, and they came out on top. You can do it as well. Entrepreneurship is about courage, and we all are blessed with a great capacity to be brave and bold.

Finally, just do it!

CHAPTER 16
CONGRATULATIONS

Congratulations on deciding to become an Entrepreneur. After all the soul-searching, planning and getting ready to start, I wish you success in your endeavors. I believe that the best way to achieve your dreams is to become an Entrepreneur. I encourage you to help others by letting them know about this book and how they can get their hands on it. Sharing is caring. We should not rise alone but help everyone around us rise.

Remember these things as you set out to start. Entrepreneurs think differently about the world around them. They are not motivated by fitting in or going with the flow. They think independently and have strong views on how their life should be lived. Entrepreneurs are not satisfied with the status quo. Their dream is to live the life that makes them happy and settling for less is discomforting.Entrepreneurs are driven and enthusiastic. They live life passionately and want the most out of life.Entrepreneurs value independence to be able to make decisions that best support their dreams and their lives.Entrepreneurs dream of Financial Freedom. This is having the resources to do the things they desire most.

Entrepreneurs will never be emotionally settled and satisfied within themselves until they have accomplished their dreams.Entrepreneurs dream of Freedom in all forms and fashions.Entrepreneurs value time and want more of it.Entrepreneurs dislike wastage and spending a life without being true to themselves is wasting their life.Many know that their purpose and calling in life is to become an Entrepreneur, it is a part of their identity and the way they are wired.Entrepreneurs feel the need to contribute something of value to society.We all desire to do something of significance, and many find that significance through entrepreneurship.This book is the first in a series of books that will be released by the author. Look out for future

Ready. Set. Start!

releases and educational resources. There is an online course available for Ready. Set. Start!

Go to www.jonathanbachew.com

www.ingramcontent.com/pod-product-compliance
Lightning Source LLC
Chambersburg PA
CBHW020425220526
45464CB00002B/569